W9-AFN-920

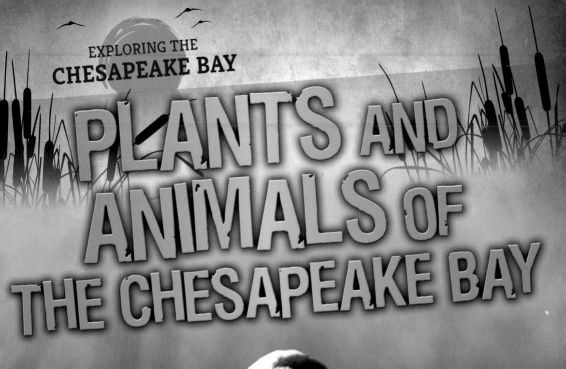

Exploring the
CHESAPEAKE BAY

PLANTS AND ANIMALS OF THE CHESAPEAKE BAY

By Kathleen Connors

Gareth Stevens
Publishing

Please visit our website, www.garethstevens.com. For a free color catalog of all our high-quality books, call toll free 1-800-542-2595 or fax 1-877-542-2596.

Library of Congress Cataloging-in-Publication Data

Connors, Kathleen.
Plants and animals of the Chesapeake Bay / by Kathleen Connors.
  p. cm. — (Exploring the Chesapeake Bay)
Includes index.
ISBN 978-1-4339-9781-5 (pbk.)
ISBN 978-1-4339-9782-2 (6-pack)
ISBN 978-1-4339-9780-8 (library binding)
1. Chesapeake Bay (Md. and Va.)—Juvenile literature. 2. Natural history—Chesapeake Bay Region (Md. and Va.)—Juvenile literature. 3. Habitat (Ecology)—Chesapeake Bay (Md. and Va.)—Juvenile literature. I. Connors, Kathleen. II. Title.
QH104.5.C45 C66 2014
917.55—d23

First Edition

Published in 2014 by
Gareth Stevens Publishing
111 East 14th Street, Suite 349
New York, NY 10003

Copyright © 2014 Gareth Stevens Publishing

Designer: Michael Flynn and Katelyn E. Reynolds
Editor: Kristen Rajczak

Photo credits: Cover, p. 1 glenda/Shutterstock.com; p. 5 Kmusser/Wikipedia.com; pp. 6, 13, 18–19 Peter Essick/Aurora/Getty Images; (inset) pp. 6-7 (main) Greg Pease/Photographer's Choice/Getty Images; p. 9 Lone Wolf Photos/Shutterstock.com; p. 10 JIANG HONGYAN/Shutterstock.com; p. 11 Photo Researchers/Getty Images; p. 12 Mark Caunt/Shutterstock.com; p. 15 Steve Bower/Shutterstock.com; p. 16 Elliotte Rusty Harold/Shutterstock.com; p. 17 Benjamin Albiach Galan/Shutterstock.com; p. 20 Tim Mainiero/Shutterstock.com; p. 21 Lee Prince/Shutterstock.com; p. 23 Miguel Andrade/Wikipedia.com; pp. 24–25 (map and symbols) Courtesy of the Integration and Application Network, University of Maryland Center for Environmental Science (ian.umces.edu/symbols/); p. 27 Susan Biddle/The Washington Post/Getty Images; pp. 28–29 US Navy photo by Chief Mass Communication Specialist Craig P. Strawser/Wikipedia.com.

All rights reserved. No part of this book may be reproduced in any form without permission in writing from the publisher, except by a reviewer.

Printed in the United States of America

CPSIA compliance information: Batch #CS13GS: For further information contact Gareth Stevens, New York, New York at 1-800-542-2595.

CONTENTS

Words in the glossary appear in **bold** type the first time they are used in the text.

BAY LIVING

Forests, wetlands, and sandy beaches surround the Chesapeake Bay. About 150 **tributaries** flow into it. And within the bay itself are shallows, oyster reefs, wetlands, and deeper open water. Together, these areas make up a vast **ecosystem** that's home to 3,600 species of plants and animals.

The Chesapeake Bay is found on the Atlantic coast between the states of Virginia and Maryland. Its **watershed** extends into Delaware, New York, Pennsylvania, West Virginia, and Washington, DC. More than 17 million people live in the Chesapeake Bay watershed—and that population continues to grow. Those living nearest the bay enjoy mild winters and warm, humid summers, which also draw lots of vacationers.

ESTUARY EXPLAINED

The Chesapeake Bay is an estuary. An estuary is a body of water that acts as a transition place between the salty ocean and the freshwater streams and rivers that flow into it. It's partially enclosed by land and contains a mixture of freshwater and salt water. In the spring, the Chesapeake Bay tends to have more freshwater in it.

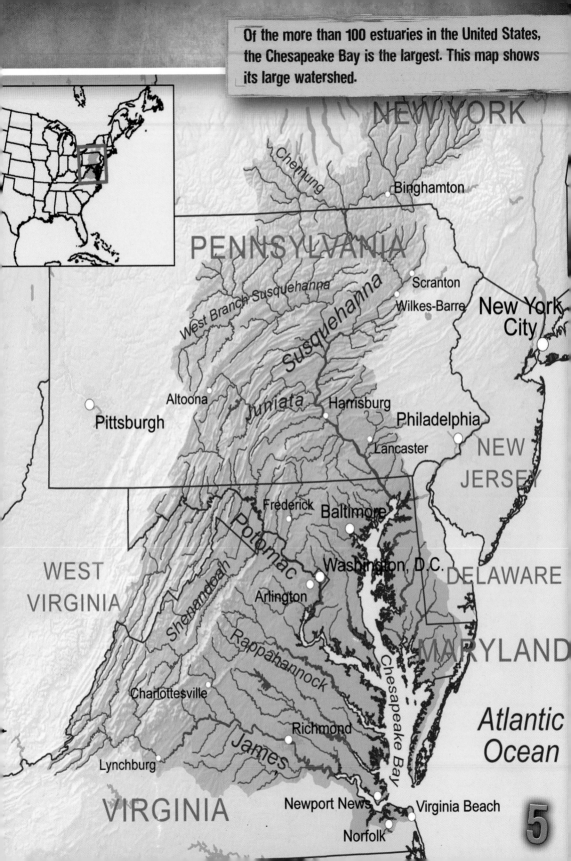

Of the more than 100 estuaries in the United States, the Chesapeake Bay is the largest. This map shows its large watershed.

NEW YORK

Chemung

Binghamton

PENNSYLVANIA

West Branch Susquehanna

Scranton

Wilkes-Barre

New York City

Susquehanna

Altoona

Juniata

Harrisburg

Pittsburgh

Philadelphia

Lancaster

NEW JERSEY

Frederick

Baltimore

Potomac

Washington, D.C.

DELAWARE

WEST VIRGINIA

Arlington

Shenandoah

Rappahannock

MARYLAND

Chesapeake Bay

Charlottesville

Atlantic Ocean

Richmond

James

Lynchburg

Newport News

Virginia Beach

VIRGINIA

Norfolk

5

The number of people who live, work, and visit the Chesapeake Bay area affects its well being, however. A growing population and booming tourism industry mean more homes, hotels, and parking lots are built over animal and plant **habitats**. Pollution has been an ongoing problem since farms were first established near the bay in the 1600s and 1700s.

Today, the 350 kinds of fish, 2,700 types of plants, as well as shellfish, waterfowl, and even microorganisms fight for their lives in the Chesapeake Bay and its surrounding **environments**. While some species have been recognized as **endangered**, others flourish in the many different habitats of this beautiful estuary.

POLLUTION IN THE HARBOR OF BALTIMORE, MARYLAND

THE BAY BY THE NUMBERS

length: 200 miles (322 km)

width: from 4 miles (6.4 km) near Aberdeen, Maryland, to more than 30 miles (48 km) near Cape Charles, Virginia

depth: 21 feet (6.4 m) on average. Many parts of it are much shallower.

surface area: including tributaries, 4,480 square miles (11,603 sq km)

shoreline length: including coastal tributaries, 11,684 miles (18,800 km)

watershed surface area: 64,000 square miles (165,760 sq km)

This highway in Baltimore, Maryland, is just one example of the way people can upset the balance of the ecosystems around the Chesapeake Bay watershed.

BLUE CRAB

A blue crab's life takes it to many habitats within the Chesapeake Bay. Baby blue crabs, or zoea, hatch in salty waters before molting, or shedding their skin, several times. They then settle on the bay's muddy bottom. Young crabs move to the bay's **brackish** waters and by adulthood make their way into tributaries, too.

These bottom dwellers prey on anything they can find, including fish, plants, and worms. Herons, sea turtles, and people are some of the predators they face. Overharvesting of blue crabs has hurt their numbers in the past. Environmental changes, such as cold winters, affect blue crab populations, too.

North America

blue crab range

South America

TAKING CARE OF BUSINESS

About 500 million pounds of seafood come out of the Chesapeake Bay each year. The blue crab is a big part of this industry. It's one of the most valuable catches that fishermen bring in. In 2008, the number of crabs that could be caught in the Chesapeake Bay was reduced to help declining crab populations. By 2011, the blue crab population had rebounded and was at its highest since 1997.

The Chesapeake Bay isn't the only place to find blue crabs. They make their homes all along the Atlantic coast and can be found as far north as Canada and as far south as Argentina.

EASTERN AMERICAN OYSTERS

Would you eat a slimy **invertebrate** right out of its shell? Many people do! In fact, the eastern American oyster found in the brackish water of the Chesapeake Bay is one of the most commonly harvested food oysters. Oysters live in colonies, or reefs. Oyster reefs were once so large and abundant in the Chesapeake Bay that boats had to sail around them!

Called filter feeders, oysters pull water into their shells and through their gills to catch **plankton** to eat. This makes them easily affected by polluted water. Overharvesting and diseases also have decreased the number of eastern oysters in the bay over the past few decades.

BENTHIC ORGANISMS

Benthic organisms are indicator species that play an important part in the Chesapeake Bay ecosystem. The health of indicator species can tell scientists a lot about the health of the bay. Benthic organisms, including oysters, clams, and bacteria, are found on the bay's bottom. They break down waste or serve as food for other animals. Since benthic organisms don't travel much, they can't move away from pollution or from **nutrient** or chemical imbalances in the water. Scientists use indicator species and other gauges to measure the health of the bay.

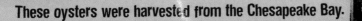

These oysters were harvested from the Chesapeake Bay.

MENHADEN

While menhaden can be found all along the Atlantic coast, the Chesapeake Bay is an important spot for this species of fish. The less salty water of the estuary is the perfect place for young menhaden to grow before they head to the ocean as adults.

Menhaden are a key link in the food chain of the Chesapeake Bay. They eat plankton and plant waste, and are prey for other fish, including striped bass and tuna. As menhaden swim together in large schools, their silvery scales can be seen above the water. This makes them easy prey for birds, such as ospreys, herons, and eagles, too.

FISHERIES

The word "fishery" means all the activities that are part of catching a kind of fish or sea creature. Commercial fisheries, like menhaden fisheries, harvest fish not consumed by humans, but instead made into products such as fish oil, feed for livestock, and bait for other fish.

Like other Chesapeake Bay sea creatures, menhaden are commonly overharvested.

BLUE HERON

Spring arrives early on the Chesapeake Bay with the clacks, howls, and growls of great blue herons nesting in the shallows of the bay and its tributaries. These huge birds breed in many places in the United States and Canada, but more than half of the Atlantic coast blue herons nest on the Chesapeake Bay. Many are year-round residents, too.

Blue herons mainly eat crustaceans and fish from the bay. They swallow food whole, including small animals and insects. Although adult blue herons grow to 4 feet (1.2 m) tall—making them the largest heron—bears, eagles, or raccoons may eat them.

WINTERING WATERFOWL

There are 29 kinds of waterfowl that make their home near the Chesapeake Bay. Each year, about 1 million waterfowl winter on the bay! It's right in the flight path of many **migratory** birds traveling along the Atlantic coast. Depending on the time of year, swans, piping plovers, and ruby-throated hummingbirds, among others, can be seen near the Chesapeake Bay.

The blue heron cannot be hunted because of the Migratory Bird Act of 1918. However, these beautiful birds do face poor water quality and habitat loss that could harm their numbers in the future.

SEA TURTLES

Thousands of leatherback, green, Kemp's ridley, and loggerhead sea turtles come to the Chesapeake Bay when the water warms up during the spring. The loggerhead, leatherback, and Kemp's ridley look for sea creatures to eat. The green sea turtle feasts on the bay's grasses and plants.

All species of sea turtle are endangered or threatened under the Endangered Species Act of 1973. "Threatened" means they may become endangered. The act makes it illegal to hunt sea turtles in the United States. Still, hundreds of turtles die each year in the Chesapeake Bay after they've been hit by boats, tangled in nets, harmed by fishing gear, or have swallowed trash.

LOGGERHEAD
SEA TURTLE

THE LOGGERHEAD

The most common sea turtle found in the Chesapeake Bay is the loggerhead. They have a big head and can weigh 150 to 400 pounds (68 to 182 kg)! Each year, a few loggerhead nests are found in the sands of Virginia Beach. However, only 1 in 100 loggerheads lives to be an adult. They're listed as a threatened species.

Female sea turtles often lay their eggs in holes they dig on the beaches of the Chesapeake Bay.

SAV

Submerged aquatic **vegetation** (SAV) is the name for all the underwater grasses that grow in the shallows of the Chesapeake Bay. There are more than a dozen types of SAV, and they don't all take root in the same place. One kind of SAV, wild celery, prefers the freshwater of tributaries, while another called eelgrass grows best in saltier water.

SAV is an important habitat for many bay animals like young fish and shellfish such as the blue crab, providing them a safe haven from hungry predators. This same habitat is also home to barnacles that attach themselves to eelgrass and many of the bay's waterfowl.

MANY IMPORTANT JOBS

SAV is more than a habitat. It helps improve water quality for all bay life. These grasses release much-needed oxygen, as well as filter particles and nutrients that can build up and cloud the water. SAV has an important role in the food chain, too. Plankton eat decaying SAV, and the plankton then become food for other species. SAV is also food for waterfowl.

All SAV grows below the surface of the water. Otherwise, it would dry out.

BALD CYPRESS TREE

Have you ever seen a tree with knees? The way the bald cypress tree's roots grow, it looks like it has knobby knees reaching out of the swampy ground where it grows! The "knees" help the tree stay in place, a task of great importance to the Chesapeake Bay area. The root system of the bald cypress trees keeps large areas of soil from eroding, or being moved away by wind and water.

Bald cypress swamps are found in the southern part of the Chesapeake Bay watershed. When the trees grow in standing water, the bottom of their trunk swells, making its shape look somewhat like a pyramid.

ROOTS OF BALD CYPRESS TREES

THE WETLANDS

Swamps, bogs, and marshes are all wetlands found around the Chesapeake Bay. These special ecosystems are usually flooded, though the amount of water depends on the area and time of year. In estuarine wetlands, salt water and freshwater mix, such as in the marshes along the bay's shore. Other wetlands contain only freshwater. Both are home to hydrophytes, or water-loving plants.

Bald cypress swamps are another kind of habitat in the Chesapeake Bay area. Turtles and snakes make their home there. Owls, bees, and ducks may nest in hollow trees.

ARROW ARUM

Named for its arrow-shaped leaves, arrow arum (EHR-uhm) has a tall stalk and little flowers that grow on a spike called a spathe. Large colonies grow in the shallow freshwater of the Chesapeake Bay. Its huge leaves, which can be 18 inches (46 cm) long, can be seen in marshes and swamps, as well as along the shores of rivers and streams.

The roots of thick growths of arrow arum help hold soil in place. Arrow arum colonies also make ideal places for waterfowl, insects, and small animals to hide. Their fruit provides food for the animals, too, and is a special favorite of the wood duck.

FUN FACTS ABOUT ARROW ARUM

- It's sometimes called tuckahoe and duck corn.

- Some Native American tribes used dried and ground arrow arum roots as flour. They would cook and eat the fruit like peas, too.

- It's a perennial, which means it grows back every year.

- Arrow arum is found as far north as Ontario, Canada, and as far south as Florida.

The arrow arum fruit—clusters of black-green berries—can be so heavy, the plant will fall over!

LIFE IN THE CHESAPEAKE BAY

The many habitats in the Chesapeake Bay include swamps, brackish water, freshwater streams, and many more—and they're full of life! Use this cutaway map to explore the environments of the plants and animals in this book.

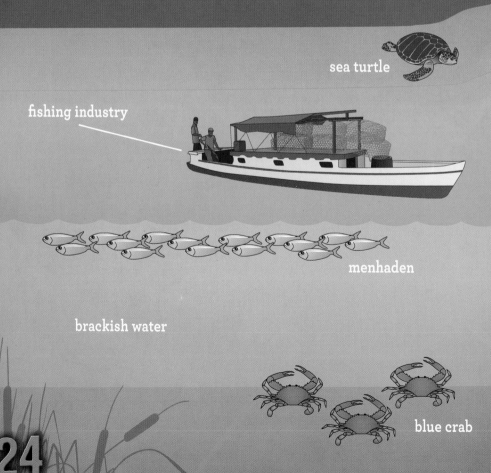

sea turtle

fishing industry

menhaden

brackish water

blue crab

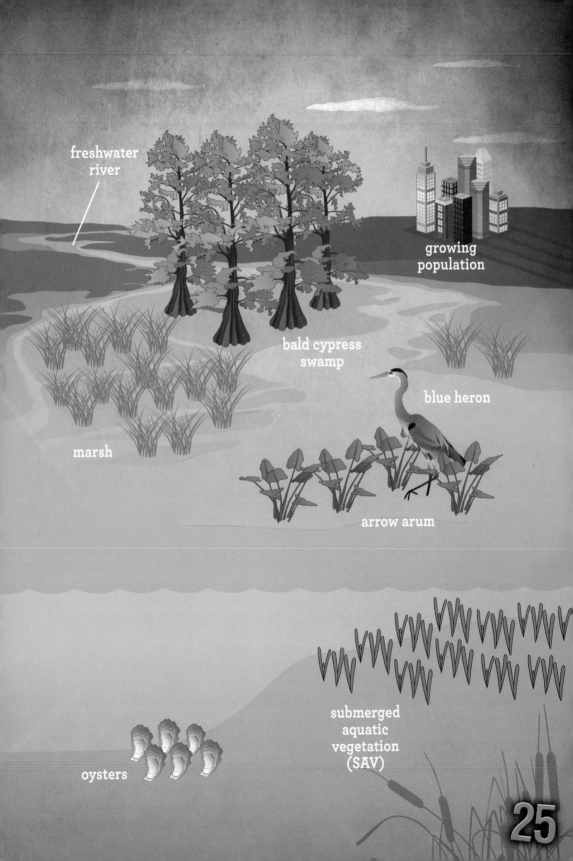

freshwater river

growing population

bald cypress swamp

blue heron

marsh

arrow arum

oysters

submerged aquatic vegetation (SAV)

25

CONSERVATION SITUATION

Conservation is a very important part of keeping the Chesapeake Bay clean and the species in it healthy and plentiful. Groups such as the National Wildlife Federation spend a lot of time and money studying ecosystems around the country that need special attention. Their work often helps pass laws limiting pollution, hunting, fishing, and construction that could harm these areas.

The Chesapeake Bay has many local groups working on just its problems, too. The Chesapeake Bay Foundation has programs, such as Clean the Bay Day, that help to restore the bay's shoreline. The foundation is also collecting oyster shells for rebuilding oyster reefs! The group tries to include the community in these projects to increase concern and knowledge of the environment.

These students are learning about conservation by looking for oyster reefs in the bay.

WHAT IS CONSERVATION?

Conservation is the protection of parts of nature, including animals, plants, and habitats such as wetlands. A person who works for conservation is sometimes called a conservationist. Conservationists often try to teach others about their cause. They want to make sure places like the Chesapeake Bay are around for people in the future to enjoy.

27

Oysters aren't the only Chesapeake Bay animal conservation groups are worried about. Efforts to increase the population of the blue crab have been underway for more than a decade. The Virginia Institute of Marine Science has a special program that helps hundreds of stranded sea turtles each year, too.

Plants and habitats have conservation support, too. In 2009, 290 acres of wetlands, including many bald cypress trees, became a protected area. But not every conservation effort has to be big! Anyone can follow the gardening guide published by the US Fish and Wildlife Service. It encourages people in the bay area to use native plants in their gardens.

GLOBAL CLIMATE CHANGE

As Earth's climates continue to slowly change, sea levels are rising. Six inches (15 cm) of the water level's rise in the Chesapeake Bay during the 20th century was an effect of global climate change. The rising water levels have already covered some of the bay's small islands. Over time, this will cause coastal habitats to change or even be lost—along with some of the plants and animals living there.

Do you want to keep the Chesapeake Bay's many plants and animals healthy? Many groups have programs especially for school groups, kids, and families who want to help.

GLOSSARY

brackish: having a mix of salt water and freshwater

ecosystem: all the living things in an area

endangered: in danger of dying out

environment: everything in an area that affects the plants or animals living there

habitat: the natural place where an animal or plant lives

invertebrate: an animal without a backbone

migratory: having a way of life that includes migrating, or moving from one area to another for the winter or breeding

nutrient: something a living thing needs to grow and stay alive

plankton: a tiny plant or animal that floats in the ocean

tributary: a stream that flows into a larger body of water

vegetation: plant life

watershed: the whole area that drains into a body of water

FOR MORE INFORMATION

Books

Dayton, Connor. *Wetland Animals.* New York, NY: PowerKids Press, 2009.

Hartman, Eve, and Wendy Meshbesher. *What Is the Threat of Invasive Species?* Chicago, IL: Raintree, 2012.

Musselman, Lytton John, and David A. Knepper. *Plants of the Chesapeake Bay: A Guide to Wildflowers, Grasses, Aquatic Vegetation, Trees, Shrubs, & Other Flora.* Baltimore, MD: Johns Hopkins University Press, 2012.

Websites

Bay Field Guide
www.chesapeakebay.net/fieldguide
Find out about even more plants and animals that live in the Chesapeake Bay watershed.

Chesapeake and Coastal Bay Life
www.dnr.state.md.us/bay/cblife/index.html
There are so many kinds of plants and animals in the Chesapeake Bay area! Find out about others on this website.

Chesapeake Bay
www.nwf.org/wildlife/wild-places/chesapeake-bay.aspx
Read about the problems facing the wildlife in and around the Chesapeake Bay and other areas in the United States.

Publisher's note to educators and parents: Our editors have carefully reviewed these websites to ensure that they are suitable for students. Many websites change frequently, however, and we cannot guarantee that a site's future contents will continue to meet our high standards of quality and educational value. Be advised that students should be closely supervised whenever they access the Internet.

INDEX